MW01526394

Healthy Connections:

Guide on Relationships

Moonsoulchild

Welcome to my **Guide on Relationships.**

I don't know all there is to know about relationships, but I know enough to give my insight. This book will be an experience, my experience. I have not been in many relationships, but I've been in enough to know the difference between when to stay and when to walk away. This book is not only about relationships, but also platonic relationships, friendships, soulmates, and family. The connections we have with everyone we love. I will give you raw, personal experiences close to my heart. I'm not telling you what's right or wrong, you choose the path that feels right for you. You will love. You will feel pain. You will go through many different emotions loving someone, whether they are right or wrong. I just hope my insight can guide you to the place of healing you are looking for. I just hope my experiences can give you another perspective. Love can be blinding, I can attest to that, but there comes a time where you need to stop excusing that behavior and open your eyes. I pray when you are reading you feel how passionate I am for everyone I love and let go, they all changed and made an imprint on my life differently. I believe that is the most important lesson, when to hold on, and when it's time to walk away.

You will never rise from a heart break,
If you soak in the pain,
Instead of planting new seeds
for growth and healing.

You ever wonder why you feel so broken? You ever feel like you are never going to find someone to love you, the same way you give love? It's because you're choosing to soak in the heartbreak instead of focusing on starting new beginnings. If you chose to dwell on the sadness and fight away happiness, pain will always be a reassurance. Turning cold does not "numb the pain" it only projects it onto everyone who tries to love you. Not everyone who walks into your life is going to hurt you, but you reject everyone who tries to get close because of the last one who hurt you. It is impossible to move on without the power of true healing. If you hide the pain and try to silence it, it will only come out another time, projected onto someone who does not deserve it. Keeping your demons in the dark will only make loving someone new harder. True love may seem out of reach.

It is important to feel every emotion going through you at every moment. If you are sad, cry. If you are mad, take a moment to breathe. If you are happy, indulge in that moment.

When you get your heart impaired it's either because someone exited your life when you thought they would be around forever, or you thought someone loved you more than they expressed. Sometimes we create our own heart break by holding onto people who are not meant to stay. We cling onto unrealistic expectations that are just illusions based on our desires. We blame everyone who walked out for our pain, because it is the easiest way to make sense of the situation.

We fight for what we believe we are losing, because we want to prove the love that flows through us is nothing less than real. We create this illusion of love based off films, books, or other relationships. We fall too much into what society has made love to be, and the opinions of everyone around us. We never understood what love truly is. Get that out of your head. Love is an emotion, something you feel, not something that needs to look a certain way. There is a huge difference between love and the means to make a relationship work.

It is one thing to love someone, but another to have a relationship. Sometimes you love someone who is not meant to be more than a moment. Sometimes a relationship is not in the cards. I believe our fate is already written and the more we go against what is for us, the more we shift away from what's important. In order to have a relationship with someone you need:

1. Communication

Communication is the most important part of a relationship. A lot of people carry tons of trust issues from past relationships and most of the time take those same insecurities into the new relationship. Communication comes in different forms. The main form is to speak about your past, tell your partner everything you have been through so there won't be any miscommunication. You cannot expect your partner to trust you without being upfront with them. **If you are scared to bring your past to light you shouldn't be in another relationship until you've made peace with it**.

Your partner deserves to know how you have been hurt, but also the hurt you placed onto others. This eliminates the possibility of those mistakes being repeated in your new relationship. I know, some may say "How do you trust someone when you have trust issues?" and truthfully, you should have an open mindset when it comes to someone new in your life, you shouldn't treat them like everyone who hurt you because you let your guard down. Treating someone like they hurt you when they have not or carrying many insecurities with you from the past will only hurt the relationship.

2. Partnership

I think working together is especially important, it helps both of you work through things together and not to let each others fire burn out. If you live together it is important to both have chores and help around the house in any way you can without making your other half take up all the work. I learned that from past relationships, I burnt myself out doing everything while they didn't do a thing. If you are a woman, you don't need to be a housewife, your partner should know it's important for you not to be over worked. It should not feel like a job to be in a relationship, your partner should feel like home, your safe place.

The key is not overextending yourself, be with someone who does not let you drown in too much responsibility. Too much stress on both ends can cause a lot of friction and cause you both to lose focus on the real meaning of love.

3. Date nights

Date nights are important. The stress of your everyday life can get overwhelming, sometimes it is hard to take a step back and see the happiness because you're blinded by short term goals, chores around the house, or your work. Pick a night that both of you can spend together doing something you both love to do. Keeping the love alive may seem hard because once you feel comfortable you soak in it so far you forget what the honeymoon phase felt like. I can attest to getting comfortable, especially in past relationships, I got bored without even knowing. I was caught up in the realm of our everyday lives I had no more energy to give to our love.

Now, every Friday is date night. We choose something to focus on and get some take out and indulge in each other. Even if it is just watching a movie or our favorite show, to going to the beach, or just out. Sometimes it is just us together learning about each other more.
 Once you find someone you share a piece of your soul with it gets easier to focus on that love over comfort, because your partner will show you the same love and attention you deserve. It will not be a thought in your head if your partner loves you because they will always provide actions that back up their love for you. The love will come naturally, a feeling of home.

What is a healthy relationship? (from my experience)

1. Falling without trying

If you are going on blind dates, using dating apps, continuing to look for someone to love you, it will always be flawed. You are forcing love to be found, you're forcing yourself to fall for someone else. Stop looking, build you. Love will find you when it is time.

2. Find yourself

Who are you?

What are your interests?

What do you love about yourself?

Do you love yourself?

If you cannot answer these questions, you're unable to give love to someone else without it being conditional.

3. Find your worth

Without self- worth you will not know what you deserve. You will keep accepting love from anyone who shows it to you.

What are you worth?

Why are you worthy?

What makes you someone, someone should love?

Why should someone be blessed to love you?

4. Do not let advice from anyone influence you

You tend to ask a friend or family for advice about love when you are stuck, but the only best-known advice is your intuition. It has important to listen to what they have to offer you, but to focus on changing your perception based off what others believe is not a good start. Everyone has experienced love and heart break in different forms, they cannot dictate what you truly feel, or know the other persons intentions. No one knows the answers but you.

5. Communication

Do not speak to speak, speak to be understood. You must have good communication. If you cannot speak about what concerns you, you won't make it. Take a moment to listen, and not to speak next but to intake what's being heard.

6. Support

You cannot be with anyone who doesn't support you or your dreams, don't try it. It will be led to constant arguments. Someone who supports you not only understands you but love yours for what you give to yourself, not just what you bring into their lives.

7.   Leave your past in the past

Do not bring old trust issues, patterns, or anything involving your pas into the new relationship. If you cannot do this, you need to rebuild yourself before starting a new relationship. It is not fair to someone new to deal with something you haven't let go of.

8.   Friendship

Starting as friends and continuing that friendship through the relationship is key. Having a friendship first builds the foundation of your relationship. If you cannot have your partner as your friend, why be with them? Falling for a friend is the purest form of love.

9.   Loyalty

It is obvious to be loyal while in a relationship, but loyalty is a character trait. If you cannot be loyal it will ruin all ties in your relationship. Having a healthy relationship with yourself should teach you to be loyal, or you will always be mistreated.

10. Knowledge of understanding

Understand you will experience bad times. At times you will feel like the world is against you. Living in fear of your own insecurities, having mutual understanding of each other's fears can help overcome any barrier you place on you or your relationship.

11. Disagreements

It is easy to get upset for something they didn't do, or that they did. It is hard to understand the difference of ways. If you do not have excellent communication skills, you won't master any disagreement. Communicate the problem to make it through.

12. Honesty

Honesty is also a character trait, which ties into communication. If you cannot communicate, you won't be honest. This comes back to working on yourself. You cannot be honest with yourself; you can't be honest with anyone.

In conclusion, if you can master all of the above, you will have a complete healthy relationship (as if your partner also shares the same view) the most important of all, is finding yourself and the worth within you. Once you are happy with yourself it will be possible to accept nothing less than what you deserve. Things like unconditional love and happiness, they come naturally when you have mastered the art of loving yourself, and the love brought to you after. You do not need to make either a priority, those things are felt and will be give every day to each other without force.

Now use the rest of the page to reflect:

Stop going back to the same person who damaged your outlook on love, who made you change your ways and turn cold. There is nothing left for you to give, or receive, it's time to leave history where it belongs.

The first step to not returning to old patterns or relationships is to focus on why you left. How was the relationship before it ended? Why did it end? If you find yourself turning to cold tendencies because you're scared to love or you're afraid to be hurt, you're going all about love wrong.

The best way to completely move forward is to leave the past where it belongs and that is behind you. Do not use love as an excuse to keep taking someone back that doesn't fit into your growth any longer. I believe people change but only if they truly wish to, and change does not happen overnight, so don't believe someone when they come back a month later.

I have been the girl who took back someone multiple times because I used love as an excuse to justify why I kept going back. I used love as an excuse to make what I kept doing feel right. I had high hopes that we would make it work each time we had, that fate kept bringing us together for another chance at love.

What I did not realize was there was no love within us, the love was only within what I held. He kept me close when he wanted me, when he needed someone to pick him up when he felt against the world. I made him feel irreplaceable. He fed off my love for him. He knew what he was doing but still played on my heart. His existence was a weapon to me, one I was afraid of because I saw him for the illusion, I based upon us, not the truth that was right in front of me.

I held myself in contempt when I realized I let myself turn cold because of someone who had no respect for me. I fell to the deepest darkest parts of myself I never once visited until he brought me there. I let good people walk in and out my life before I could have a chance to see what they could give me.

I could not love another at this point because I was too focused on what I lost and what could possibly hurt me in the future. I had a wall up so tall, a guard up so tough, no one was able to break through. It was the feeling of loneliness I hated the most. I did not like feeling cold, I had too much love to give to let myself freeze.

So, let me say,

- **Do not rush back to what brought pain**

Turning back to comfort because it is all you know won't change a thing. If the universe brought you two apart there is a good chance that's how it was meant to go on. You tend to ask yourself why they come into your life to only hurt you, because I have been there, and I've blamed myself countless times. Sometimes we love people that never stay and that is one of the hardest pillows to swallow.

Learning to let go of someone who you grew to love but did not love you back, it breaks your heart. So, you take them back again to prove to yourself the pain was not for anything. That it may have not been your time, but don't let history repeat and you lose yourself.

"Just because you love someone,
spent years being with, or a friend to,
does not mean you need them in your life.
It is possible to love from afar.
It is possible to love and let go".

I know it feels wrong to let someone go after promising to love them forever, but you cannot hold someone against their growth just to keep them in your life. Or to hold yourself back from growing, for that matter. Who outgrows who is not the case, it's the continuance of trying to chase what's faded, or the need of mending what we can't see as broken because we're too busy fantasizing what we want. History does not always need to be repeated. History does not mean consider letting people stay more than they're welcomed by your heart.

Do not stay because it's familiar, you'll always get familiar pain. After time, the love lost will hurt less, once you realize it was best to set them free. Love will always be felt, even after a disastrous ending, what you once felt was real, that does not change.

I had a friend I grew with until my 20's. The memories were unforgettable. The pain has healed within time. The love I have is still within my heart, but I have come to realization we weren't meant to grow together, only apart.

"Do not be afraid to try again,
To love again,
Not everyone is bad for you.
Stop choosing so easily,
Make them prove they are worthy of your love."

There are souls out there, one, who's looking for their twin flame. Then there is you, who's hiding within insecurities and the blockage of confidence at love because the pain has shielded you for too long. You put up a good fight, but then sometimes let people in too easily. Not everyone is bad for you, so it is unfair to place blame onto someone who didn't even have the chance to hurt you, let alone love you. Stop taking away chances from people who never got close because of the demons you are carrying, not because they hurt you.

Instead of blocking love,

- **Set boundaries**

Setting boundaries will help give you balance. It will help condition the love that comes along. People in your past may have gotten away with things when you had your guard down, but that does not mean anyone who comes next has to pick up the pieces.

You either,

1. **Let the pain change you**

If you chose to soak in the heart break, you are choosing to let it change your way of thinking and loving. You start picking up cold hearted behavior, using your head more and your heart less. You are starting to hurt those who come along because you treat them with the same disrespect others have treated you. I know it hurts to let your heart open back up once someone hurt you, but it is important to stay warm during the time you're most vulnerable.

2.   Let the pain shape you

It took me awhile to reach this level of confidence but now that I have arrived, I can't go back. I let pain shape me instead of defining me. When I let it define me, I let it control my every part of thinking and feeling. I realized it is impossible not to feel, because even when I let go of my want of love, I became victim of pain and sadness and let it feed off me. Facing the pain head on without giving up, even when your heart gets heavy, it brings you to a place of pure bliss.

Moral of the story,

Make them prove they are worthy of your love. Get rid of them if they play on your heart, you are love.

"Do not stay in an unhealthy relationship
because you love someone, chances are,
They do not love you as much as you love them.
You should not have to overextend yourself
to prove that your love is rare.
If they do not feel it,
It is not for them,
Keep your heart safe."

The worst thing you can do is stay in an unhealthy relationship without knowing you are being taken advantage of because you don't know your worth. Being blinded by love is real, and once you fall too deep in you will find yourself excusing their behavior, and when it comes to how they treat you.

You cannot expect anyone to treat you with the same love and respect you give if you're letting them walk in and out your life when they please. People will treat you exactly how they know they will get away with, this means taking what they need and fulfilling their needs without thinking of the pain you'll be left with. I can't piece together the other beings actions to make sense of the puzzle, but I can speak on the insecurities they're holding close, but when they're with you, they let you hold the weight and try and fix them.

Love is not undoing someone's pain. Love is accepting someone as they are and for what they bring into your life, and how they inspire you to be a greater you. Love isn't a constant chase for being what someone needs, or to prove the love you have is sacred because it's rare. it's how precious it is and how you keep it safe out here, so you can share it with someone who truly provides not only care, but stability.

"You will love the worst kind of hearts
throughout your lifetime, one thing is,
You will love them for a reason,
There is always a purpose.
Not everyone will be
someone who is meant to stay,
When the bad takes itself out the story,
Stop blaming yourself."

You will meet people throughout your life, many people who you will love, and not all of them will be someone worth remembering. Some will spark love but then end in pain, as you remember them as the worst hearts to come by. Do not dwell on the "what if" that could have been. Soak in what they taught you about love, the ups and downs.

There is a purpose with every soul who passes in and out your life. The purpose may not be the one you wished, but it is one you needed. When a love story comes to an end stop blaming yourself for everything that went wrong. Stop blaming yourself for the unknown. If the bad takes itself out the story and you are living a happier, more positive life, don't blame yourself for being happy.

People with big hearts have the most trouble with trying not to hurt someone's feelings even when they are no longer committed to them. People with big hearts have trouble with hurting anyone, even after having pain inflicted upon them. They take the precautions of not hurting them in return. The worst kind of hearts are the ones who bring pain into your world than try and play victim, the ones who do not grow with you, so they try and stunt your growth.

"Let those hearts that roam find their
destination,
They hurt you, they let you go,
There is a reason, a bigger purpose,
Move on."

"When you are rare,
People want to keep you close
Even if that means loving the idea
Of what they have made of you,
Not actually giving you
The love you are worthy of.
People will take advantage of your good heart
Knowing you will stick around,
So, they play with how far you will go."

"We have all loved someone
Who wasn't good for us,
It is not a mistake,
So, do not regret it.
It taught us that loving them
Was only a lesson on what love isn't
And the love we deserve is still out there."

"Do not let anyone who once hurt you
Make you believe you were the pain.
If you caused some,
We all make mistakes,
You are not a bad person
For choosing the road best for you.
Do not let past mistakes
Poison you with their victim behavior."

"I was afraid to let go,
Until I saw the beauty in it.
I was stubborn
When it came to leaving anyone I loved behind,
Until I saw disloyalty on their part.
It was not until I stepped outside myself,
I saw the real in them.
I was making excuses
When I should have been walking away."

"When someone loves you,
Their actions should always speak louder.
You should not have to wonder if they love you,
You should feel comfort knowing
They are keeping you safe from the world
While loving you unconditionally."

If you must ask yourself if they love you, it's more than likely they don't. If you are desperately trying to find answers to a situation that should not be a mystery, it's time to look the other way. The hardest part is trying to see the real in someone after you invested time and love into them. Everything you feel enables every lie, every feeling that goes against your better judgment. You start to believe the lies. You start to believe the illusion you made of something that never existed.

We all have fell deeply for someone based on a lie. We fall for the thought of being in love, without knowing the person completely. I never understood someone who had a different partner every month, but I did realize it was because there was a void to fill, which left them empty every so often. To love someone, you need to know their deepest secrets, even if they are dark, even if they may scare you away. You need to know everything there is to know of the person you are investing your world in.

Ask them,

- **What are your goals?**
- **What are your fears?**
- **What are your dreams?**
- **What is the darkest place your mind has gone?**
- **What was your happiest moment?**

Pick their brain. Do not be afraid to ask questions and ask anything that you believe you should know. Remember, you are going to share a world with this soul, you deserve all of them. Don't be discouraged if you hear something you didn't wish to know. Don't let it cloud your judgment (unless they murdered or raped someone). We all have a past and sometimes it's not pretty. So, do not judge, accept them for who they are.

Now the important part is how they treat you, too. Are they taking the time to learn all of you? Keep your eyes open, because a lot of us tend to become blind in the honeymoon phase and then wonder why things changed.

The honeymoon phase is the phase that seems to end for many, they become comfortable in routine and lose the love and intimacy that started the relationship. It is an on-going debate whether the honeymoon phase is a phase, or if it's something you can keep ongoing forever. I believe it is forever.

So, listen,

You meet someone and connect instantly. You both have undeniable chemistry. You spend days getting to know all the in's and outs of each other. You have a couple of sleepovers, and maybe even end up together quicker than you thought. I am speaking from my experience, I have been here, and the honeymoon phase is different in a lot of relationships.

I was searching for love most of the time or chasing the idea. I thought I could heal anyone who was hurt and love them, without knowing their worth, or mine for that matter. The chemistry is high, and nothing feels wrong, until you're a year in and you feel off. What is scary is when you are investing energy into another human's heart and you realize everything from their past has reoccurred into your relationship. I tried to separate myself from the past many times, but it always came to haunt me.

I did not realize how hard it was to be with someone who was not yet a founder of themselves, but also hasn't let go of pain from their past or love from the ghost of their many lovers. It's completely terrifying to know that things may change in the years to come, but if you look closely and are a high believer in trusting your intuition, you'll see the signs as they come. It's important to not dead them once they arrive, they're more meaningful than you know. It will save you a lot of hurting if you realize when it is presented.

I know it may seem like a lot, to live in the moment but to also guard your heart, but it will save you from the many souls who are not meant to overstay their welcome. The honeymoon phase never ends, the only comfort you will feel is the safeness they bring, along with their unconditional love.

People will stay in relationships they outgrew and expect happiness to come from it. Nothing good will come from something that is no longer in the cards. The more you force the more the relationship becomes toxic on both ends. One sees the other already walked away emotionally but decides to fight because they love them. The other decides to hold onto them because they do not want to hurt them, yet searches for attention elsewhere, when it could easily be resolved with communication.

A piece of advice,

If you aren't happy, let your partner know. They are aware, or may not be, but holding onto them is confusing them. The pain you bring upon them will overcome, but the longer you hold them close the more toxic the relationship will become. I don't believe toxicity just comes in physical abuse. I believe the biggest toxicity comes from mistreating yourself, which creates toxicity in the one you love or wish to set free. Always playing victim does not make you a good person, especially if you cannot be accountable. You cannot be scared to let someone go because you do not want to hurt them. You are hurting them more by holding on knowing you do not love them anymore.

"People will stay in unhappy relationships forever and somehow find their opinion valid when you choose to find happiness outside of the relationship you outgrew."

"Some people do not understand the concept of love and happiness because they are blinded by the toxic."

I am living proof,

Fighting for love does not always get you love, instead, it gives you perspective, a change of direction and the capability to let go when it is time. Many people have said "you should always fight for what you love, if you truly love them you should work through it."

Let me tell you a story,

I met this boy when I was sixteen, not physically because we lived in different states. We had mutual friends. Our main source was communication. He got me where he wanted me, as I gave in, he knew I would always be there.

It is sad he learned my heart early on just to abuse it. He held me close with his words that I believed had meaning. He made me feel something I never felt, I was sixteen, love was all I wanted. He saw me exactly for who I was trying to be. I fell for the game, I fell for the fool.

He kept me where he wanted me for for years. I fought for something I could not even explain, only I felt something special for him, something I did not see myself giving up. I thought he felt the same for me. We met physically when I was nineteen, he was twenty. We stayed together for 3 months, long distance. He would come stay with me for the weekends, sometimes weeks on end. This time together showed me his true colors. I learned who he was, was not who I loved. I was oblivious to the signs; he came to stay with me just to go to his friends to get high and party. Even kissed a girl he considered his "sister" and they both faked it for me. I tried hard keeping us together because I loved him, but I spent so much time trying to make us real.

I know what you are thinking,

I was sixteen, how did I know what love was? I did not, but I sure knew what love wasn't. I thought fighting for him meant love would surface the way I always thought it would. I was high off the words he spoke until actions could not back them up.

So please,

1. **Everyone who walks in your life is not someone who will be in your life forever.**

People are meant to pass in and out. We are meant to love and let go. We collect lessons throughout our lives we take with us years to come. The most important, is to not hold close attachments to everyone who is just a moment.

2. **Do not be blind to the signs, the universe always shows up, it never does wrong by you.**

If someone is showing signs of disloyalty, disrespect, or making you think you are wrong. It is not worth fighting for. They have disconnected and you cannot fight what's only felt by you, there's nothing to save. Choose to save yourself instead.

3. **Just because at one moment in life people always fought for "love" does not mean you have to, too.**

Not everything has to be a fight. Love is not a battlefield. It's not a prize you win. Love is an emotion you feel, one you will always feel. Stop attaching love to pain.

4. No relationship is perfect

There will be disagreements and arguments but when it comes down to trying to keep together what keeps falling apart, that is the universe opening your eyes to the road you should travel. Stop going against fate.

Fighting for love does not make you strong, especially when it is proven you're the only one fighting. What is strong is giving all you could, accepting you do not have control over everything. Knowing when to let go and understanding that does not stop you from loving.

I have had people ask me about long distance
relationships,

The first time I fell deeply for someone was
eight years ago. We met through Myspace. We
lived two hours away from each other. He lived
in New York and I lived in Connecticut. We had
mutual friends. We did not meet in person until
the third year knowing each other.

Before we met it was like I chased, and every
piece of him he gave, I ran with.

Throughout the time, I got to know the version
of him he led me to believe. I got to know the
love I had for him. Throughout the time, I was
blinded by what he kept feeding me and taking
everything, I had to offer. At the time, it was my
heart and he led me to -believe it was love.

Two years of chasing trying to prove my love.
Feeling high off the thought of loving someone.
Being at the need of another. I felt happy
knowing I was someone is something, I did not
care I wasn't someone's everything. I was young
but open, I took every chance at love, but I was
still cautious, just a bit blinded by a narcissist
who perfected in faking.

To reflect on that part of my life, I can only bring up one moment that brought true bliss, expect the honest moment on the bus, everything else was a blur. Every other piece of us was broken, a complete lie.

If you asked me seven years ago, I would attempt to do a long-distance relationship, I would say never again. I had the worst experience while holding this illusion until I finally could not unsee the flaw. I could not trust someone that far again.

I wasted money.
I wasted my pureness on him.
I wasted my energy entertaining the one who gave me a run for my money.
I wasted good days being sad.

What I did not waste was my time, every moment I tried, cried, or gave more, I do not regret. I came to conclusion of what love is not supposed to feel like. I learned the sadness of watching someone I love, not love me back. I saw the disloyalty upfront. I never understood my purpose to them, when all they did was show me the opposite of what they promised me. I never wasted a moment, because I realized even though I wasted things I can never take back, I gained a higher purpose. I gained a blessing from a disaster.

From seven years ago till July 10, 2018, I found myself in a long-distance relationship again. We were only distant for a month, known each other for two before (as friends). We were the best of friends as we were learning each other. It was different this time around, I felt something undeniable. I found myself wanting only him, my mind would not stop predicting. My heart would not let me believe this was not for me. I found myself doing things I never would have imagined.

I flew out to Florida to spend a weekend with him, to see if there could be more between us than just friends. I was in a relationship before him, which ended shortly before I chose to go. My life was a mess at this moment. Everything that went down was meant to.

When I tell you, everything pulled me into his direction, I am not lying. Everything with him felt right, I had no fear. It was my first time traveling alone and going on a plane. Loving him was easy, I was bold to give up everything that gave me comfort to be with someone everyone said I did not know.

Listen,

Getting to know someone from afar is the beauty in love. The love without the touch. The love you feel in your soul. My heart connected with him before my body did. My mind connected with his before I got the chance to show him affection. I loved him before I met him. We were long distance for a month, he decided to move to Connecticut, and we began our lives together. We have been together for almost two years. Our love is the strongest love I have ever felt. I find myself always thinking about how we met and how we fell. How we continue to grow in love.

Some advice,

After of what seems like a waste of your time, don't give up. Don't turn your heart from everyone because of a bad experience. If you get that feeling you cannot get rid of, explore it. Let it grow. Long distance love is not a love that should be unknown, I think it is beautiful.

Love is between two hearts, that create one beautiful soul. Distance cannot stop you from loving, it is when the loyalty doesn't make that love is when you start questioning it.

<u>Just because someone was not loyal to you does not mean they can't be loyal to someone else.</u>

Sometimes we force love. Sometimes we force something that is not meant to be. Not everyone you once loved is a terrible human, they just were not a match for you.

Someone told me that cheating is a character trait and that you cannot undo it, once a cheater always a cheater. This logic is flawed. it's selfish to think people can't evolve just because they hurt you. I cheated once. I was young and hurt. My partner at the time told a girl he was texting I was ugly in person and only looked good with makeup. My first reaction was to hurt him back, so I did. He never knew, even to this day he does not.

I told myself I was wrong, I felt guilty after making the mistake, but I did not feel bad enough to expose myself because I felt he deserved it. How could you love me but not think I am naturally beautiful?

I ended up with him for three years.

I was twenty, young and lost. This relationship started off wrong, which I did not see the many red flags. I wanted to save him from his pain. I wanted to be loved. Instead, I ended up with a lot of anxiety and insecurities more than ever.

I became toxic the moment I knew I decided to hurt him back instead of walking away. I did not love myself then, and clearly, he didn't love me like he said he did. I stayed because he was all I knew in that moment. I was someone who did not love myself.

I made the decision I thought was right and I do not regret it. I would not do it again and I didn't after I made the mistake the first time even though he didn't deserve my loyalty.

I learned at twenty-five how precious I am. I found the love I needed for so long. I set the foundation of the love I deserved, and I received it in return. I would not ever cheat again. When you are treated right, loved unconditionally, and know your worth you'll never cross that line.

I don't believe everyone who cheated will cheat again, that's it's embedded in their character. People make mistakes, it is a growing journey. If you keep repeating old patterns, it is a sense of emptiness.

Change is inevitable, but growth is a choice.

"The last time I ignored a sign the universe gave,
I ended up four years into a relationship.
Sometimes things are meant to be,
Only for some time.
If the universe keeps sending you the same signs,
Do not ignore them.
Things do not go bad for no reason,
Remember that."

I never had the desire to be friends with an ex

Reflecting on the beginning of the relationship before I was woke, how terribly I was a fool. The first sign I should not have pursued the relationship but my heart thought loving someone was a need.

I chased, I let my heart become a weapon against me. I did not have boundaries. I refused to see the red flags because I created love even when it was not healthy.

I went in the direction wherever I thought was love, or where love could grow. I confused lust with love many times and could not get passed "everything happens for a reason" just to let someone go.

I held on even when the signs turned against me, when words were spoken but never heard. I loved hard and one thing I never grasped was the meaning of loving and letting go. I had to show I loved hard; I knew that would make someone love me back.

The chase, the race of trying to make someone see my love was exhausting. I felt relieved when I could make them love me. I felt like a superhero when I saved them from their hurt and proved my love could heal them.

After all the chasing, the saving, we are at the finish line sharing this moment of "love" I created. It does not feel as good as I thought. I did not have love inside me any longer, it turned to comfort. To routine, more like friends.

I did not know my purpose; I did not know what I wanted from a relationship other than being loved. I could not tell you what I loved about myself. I could not condition the love. I have done this everytime I fell for someone until I opened my eyes and saw what was missing. I slept on myself I lost complete sight.

In my past, I fell hard two times and neither, to this day, do I wish I kept them as friends. Both relationships were created off my need for love. I did not love them for who they were because if so, I would still be there. The dark that became light proved I did not love them for everything they are.

I held pain in my heart but also brought pain too. I ended up hurting, but only as a defense on my heart from being hurt first. If I would have walked away when the sign first presented, I would have. My karma was to feel pain and relief at the same time.

I never regret the love I gave, even though it was not real without foundation, without the love for myself. I just wish I did not have to hurt someone to choose myself. The pain that never left because we were blinded by habit, change brought pain. I ended up unfulfilled because I had no purpose. I saved and proved and did not know what else to do. I convinced myself there was love but it was never enough.

I stayed in both relationships over a year, or more, with a hole in my soul because my purpose was not chasing and saving. I was tired. I always had good intentions and followed with a heavy, yet big heart, but also walked away, ghosted and brought the same heartache I felt.

I did not bring pain because I was malicious or because I did not love them. I was no longer happy and when my purpose in their life was no longer needed, I stayed longer than I was welcomed. It became toxic, our love became tainted. We became lost.
So yes,

It is normal to hurt someone without having the intention. I never meant to bring heartache to anyone I ever loved. Even though I never conditioned the love, the love that grew left meaning on my heart.

I stepped away from people who I gave my whole life to, who I dedicated time I could have found myself, which could have brought real love without the pain. The pain opened my eyes to stop the same cycle of purpose I was trying to fulfill.

I become toxic to myself keeping myself away from growing in the direction without ones I loved, but the continued signs showed they were not good for me. Having a big heart almost broke me, in the end it only built me. I could not have found a version of me without the pain.

I had many soulmates pass through whom I loved, and they lived their purpose. The love is forever pumping through my heart. The memories are the pieces I needed, good and bad, to find peace.

I no longer force what is not in the cards. It took a lot of patience, but I learned the importance of letting go. It took a lot of tears to understand no longer loving them does not mean I never did. Deciding not to drown when it came to choose.

I am not sorry I chose me,
I pray you do not hold me in vain,
And one day pray for me too.

You try every chance you get to not feel alone,
So, you settle for "love" created from a mix
Of lust and loneliness,
Only to find yourself more alone than ever.
Stop giving your soul
To the ones
who cannot even get passed your heart.

Protect your heart,
But do not protect it so much you pass up every
chance of love that comes your way.
Do not treat everyone like they hurt you,
They do not deserve to hold your old pain.
Love people as they are,
Your soul is the place most sacred,
Not everyone will open your soul,
Cherish the ones who make it through.

It is not only about love, it's about someone who supports your passion, who believes in you and cares to keep you safe from this scary world.

It is a natural feeling, to love, but there's ones who can fake that love. One thing that cannot be faked, is being meant for you, that's a given.

The words "I love you" have been used wrong many times, said when it's not meant. Those three words do not hold as much meaning to the world as much as they should. People have the wrong idea of love. People fake love you. It is easy to say I love you. It is not easy to fake someone being proud of you, making you happy, or keeping you safe.

It is important to not rush into love. Love is not those three words, it's the actions behind them. When someone loves you, they will show you without telling you first. When someone loves you, everything they do is out of love.

Stop searching for love,
I have been there,
I have searched, chased
And always came up short.

Sometimes it is best to let go when you can still hold the good of someone without creating too much pain. So, in memory, you always remember the times they brought the most to your life, those are the times most valued.

Do not wait
Until someone's life is over to support them.
You will end up feeling guilty
Whether you were there enough
Or could have done more.
Latching onto anything that contains memory.

Support people you love,
Let them know they are loved while alive,
They need it the most now more than ever.

When you have people around you who help
you grow, the ones who help you find you,
those are the ones you need around.

Surround yourself with the ones who want to see you win just as much as you want to.

If I grow and you cannot adapt to my growth,
You were not a true friend.
Being a friend is knowing through the years
We evolve,
Supporting happiness,
Also, a shoulder to cry on.
If your growth is stunted,
My happiness makes you hesitant,
I will outgrow you.

Love is beautiful when it is not forced.
The connection becomes an unbreakable bond,
The chemistry is out this world
And the sex is phenomenal.
Love created off a friendship is something more,
It is a soulmate.

One thing lacked in my previous relationships was the ability to connect with my partners on an emotional level. None of them were open enough to speak their fears, feelings or madness. Instead, they shut me out. Being an over expressive emotional soul, I could not adapt.

I am too intuitive. I like to speak how I feel. It helps me through every situation. I might need some time to reflect, but I never let the situation disappear without communicating through it. My past is opposite, I held so much in because of it.

It is hard loving someone but not fully expressing that love. I became trapped in my own mind to the point I cried more than anything. I was confused. I lost the ability to express myself being with someone who was so cold.

To them, I am toxic. They do not understand why I left; they ran with their own version of the story.

To me, I detached from us because I could not connect or absolutely love wholeheartedly. I was not appreciated for everything I am.

A word of advice,

Anyone that is in a relationship with someone who doesn't care to hear you out or thinks your "too" emotional, don't stick around. It is not good for you to hold in everything you feel to make them satisfied. Let them find someone as emotionless as them.

I wish I followed my own advice instead of trying to make every pass by acquaintance a connection.

<u>Unable to be freely you will create boundaries with</u> yourself in ways you cannot love in the amount you wish to, nor will it hold any relationship together of two souls that aren't meant to be.

Relationships, family, and friends,
It does not matter the label.
Anyone in your life that cannot communicate with you won't fully understand you,
Or love you the way you deserve.

I want you to stop searching for your soulmate,
They are not out there to be found.
They are meant to align with you
When the universe believes you need them
most.
To teach you and love all together.
Be mindful,
Not all who stop in are meant to stay.

Sometimes you do not need to search, the universe will place the right people at the right time. Everyone who makes you feel something is never wrong timing. I will not speak for your feelings, but if it's not matching, don't force it.

I once said "they're the one" as I tried hard to make it true. I convinced myself it was and ended up hurt.

Remember,

Just because the universe brought you together does not mean it can't take you apart. There is a lot of lessons people bring into our lives.

Sometimes people are brought into our lives to show us how much we can love, to test our strength and build us up for that heart wrenching heart break. Or the inseparable love. It teaches us. It is to help us grow into this beautiful soul we wish to see in everyone we love. I think it is worth remembering that.

I have loved a lot of people in my life, we come across many souls, create many connections. It all comes back to who we are. You could love the first person you meet but that does not mean you'll be with them. We feel different emotions for many different reasons. If we all hard it figured out so early, the trill would be lost. Of course, loss and heartbreak are the last we wish to feel, but it shapes us. It builds our character. If you love them, love them. When that moment is over, let it be.

Soulmates aren't just lovers,
So please,
Stop fantasizing that.
Soulmates are souls that come in your life
And touch your soul in ways no one ever did.
They made you feel something.
Even after they exit life,
You'll still hold that love.

Everyone has their definition of a soulmate. Some believe it's only one person you meet in your life and you'll be with them forever. I thought this too at one point in my life until I educated myself by letting people walk in and out of my life.

Everyone who walks in your life isn't a soulmate. Someone who gives you a feeling you never felt, who opens your soul, not just your heart. Some people don't even make it past your heart. You love them but it's nothing out of ordinary. To love someone is one thing, because loving someone comes easy, it's in our nature to love.

When we spend most of our time getting to know someone, to spending years with them, or as friend. You grow this love for them it makes it hard to walk away. One thing about love, it stays. It doesn't go anywhere. The love you held for them will forever be embedded in your heart, like an imprint of a reminder of a moment in time where your love captivated someone, maybe even helped direct them to their healing.

It's one thing to love, but it's another to have a connection. You can love someone and have chemistry, because honestly, how could love be possible without chemistry? I believe chemistry and connections are different.

Let me explain,

I had friends throughout the years I was close to and loved very much, but we didn't connect on every level. There was always something missing. I used to believe opposites attract. Now, not so much. I believe it's possible to be friends with someone who doesn't hold all your same interests, that's the balance. Too much of a distance between you will only drive you apart. I had two best friends who are no longer in my life. I met them both in high school.

One was my best friend since freshman year of high school. We met in our English class. We instantly connected because of our sense of humor. She was clown and her energy was always upbeat and a good time. Her home life was not the greatest, I won't go into detail, but she ended up staying with me for some time until she had to move away and change schools. In high school we were inseparable. If you saw me, she was always with me every chance we had. Everyone knew we were best friends. Over the years that we were split apart we tried to hold the friendship together by having sleepovers and making sure we made time for each other. It was hard of course, being a teenager without a license trying to hold together a long- distance friendship, on top of losing my best friend in this huge school where I felt like an outcast.

We kept in contact; she was close to my family. She met my grandparents before they passed, they loved her like she was their grandchild too. She loved them just as much. It was a blessing to have someone that close.

Life got difficult when it came to college. I was going to night school at a community college and she was going to school an hour away. I got into a relationship and that relationship sucked most of my life away. We became distant for about three years.

We rekindled our friendship summer of 2018. The crazy part is every time we got together it never felt different. We always had the same vibe We were more than best friends; we were sisters. I was excited to be spending more time catching up with her, seeing what life has been like since we last spoke. We spent the summer partying like there was no tomorrow.

My life transitioned being in a relationship for three years that I spend all my moments with him and nothing else but work and his family events. I barely saw my family. He never wanted to be around anyone. He never met half of them. So, don't mind me if I wanted to be free for a moment and enjoy the moment of clarity I have been blinded from.

Not too long after, I started a relationship with Michael. I made a promise to myself I would never let anyone take me away from my family or the ones who mean most to me. I love Michael because he never makes me choose. He's outgoing and incredibly soft hearted. My family welcomed him with open arms, as he adores them just as much. I'm thankful to have a relationship that doesn't affect me or the relationships I have with others.

Our relationship was growing, Michael and I decided to get our own place. My friend was sleeping over every weekend. 2018 was a summer to remember, many laughs, great times, endless memories.

Things got weird when she decided to distance herself from me, when she stated she didn't want to be around me and him. It made her feel sad. She would talk about girl's trips, and other options to hang out with just us. I would make time for her when he was at work, but that wasn't enough.

There was so much jealously stemming from her it was hard to forget. One minute she wants to come around, the next minute she's starting a whole deal. It was hard to please, and to be honest, I wasn't standing around for it. I never made her feel less. I never made her uncomfortable. If she felt uncomfortable, she could have voiced her concern. There was never any communication, just facebook posts that spoke of me. I'm 26 years old, I don't have time to wonder if I'm good enough or whether I'm pleasing someone. I'm too old to act like we didn't grow 12 years of friendship to act like we're strangers.

I became a businesswoman. I was dealing with working part time, on top of managing myself and selling books. I needed time for myself too. She didn't understand my life came with a lot. She's a party girl who doesn't work. Her past traumas always came to haunt her. I couldn't save her. I stopped trying. I just wanted us to be the sisters we were, but my growth made it hard. She changed but refused to grow. She couldn't accept my life, I couldn't keep giving myself to someone who wasn't proud of my success, or happy for entire being.

We grew a part.

Next was my best friend I met my junior year of high school. We met through a mutual friend. We connected off an awkward first meet but were close ever since. Maybe it's just the old days I miss, but   high school was a time I don't think anyone takes seriously. We all don't believe we'll make it out with the same friends. I did, and I was thankful. We had 7 good years of friendship before we came to an end.

Today, when I think of her, I think of all the good moments we shared. I can't forget those times and I believe they're the most important. I once was bitter towards our ending because I wasn't mature enough to know outgrowing is unchangeable. I'm now in a place where I can speak with the highest regards.

Our ending hurt the most, I was finding myself. I was in a new relationship (one she helped me find) and life was different for me. Unlike her, she had already experienced a real relationship. I was the shy girl who never had the voice to open about anything. She was the opposite of me, extremely outgoing and knew what she wanted. She did anything to get what she wanted, one thing I admired most about her. She was dedicated to what she loved and who she loved.

Our differences are what I believed brought us together. When we spent time together everything just felt right. There was no forcing, it was a natural connection. I believe she was a soulmate tie.

I was in college while working two jobs. I lived with my boyfriend at the time. There wasn't much time we spent together once our life's after high school kicked off. We both had our schedules and they never matched up. We always spoke about making plans, but they never went through.

I know what you're thinking,

If you love someone you make time for them. I guess we didn't try hard enough. Every time we tried something else came up. One thing I can attest to, is the fact we were always there for each other when we needed each other most. I would drop anything to make sure she was good. I was there for her college graduation. I was there when she had her first child. I was the God mother to her child. I was there for the saddest moments, her brother passing and her dad's absence, to her boyfriend cheating. Over the years we cried a lot, laughed a lot, and lived together. So many good memories, and some I wish I could forget.

I don't know when it all started, but time wasn't in our favor. Maybe it was the stress of what society believes a friendship is, or that I just wasn't enough anymore. Everytime we tried to keep us going, something always came to show us why it wasn't going to work.

It was like every chance she could, she ruined us. She would say I copied her by having freckles, like the same artists. Or simply writing a book, which was always my dream. Our friendship became more of a competition and I didn't understand. I couldn't comprehend why I was the outsider when I was always there. I never felt like I was good enough, she made it clear I wasn't.

We stopped being friends three times and every time I was the one who rekindled us. I was always the bigger person. I loved her very much, I didn't want to see her out of my life. We grew together and I wanted us to always grow as we spoke about. This ending was a start of my healing journey. Once I opened my eyes and saw the pettiness and the disrespect, it was clear to me. I decided to ghost her one day, because even after we spoke about what troubled us and how we were going to work through it, we were always a step behind.

It's been three years since I ignored her text message of her trying to one up me. I don't know if it was intentional, I'm sure it's because she was not happy with herself or where she was at, but I don't want to make excuses for her behavior. I took accountability for mine. She has not reached out. She's completely off social media. I had a dream about her telling me how unhappy she is, I woke up wishing I could check on her. God had other plans. So, I pray for her because her soul and mine are forever connected. The love I have is still strong, but I don't hurt myself over trying to make a relationship work between us. We were meant to love each other from afar. I just hope she feels this too.

I hope that was enough for you to understand just because your soul is eternally connected to them, you don't need a relationship. It's life.

You won't have just one soulmate.
There's many that stop in and change your life,
For the good,
For the bad.
Remember their impact on you.
Soulmates are ones who bring you into the
direction of growth,
Some don't make it to the next part of life with
you.

The most dangerous kind of friend,
Is the person who pretends to be a friend,
but also plays the enemy.

A soulmate is someone who walks in your life
and makes you feel something,
An undeniable connection,
An authentic feeling.

A soulmate is someone who can also walk out.
We have many soulmates,
All are meant to remain,
But they all were meant to make us feel.

"Not everything is your fault,
You don't deserve to always take the blame.
When it's your fault,
Own it.

Don't change your heart because someone
didn't deserve you.

Your love is special,
Handle it with care."

"I opened my heart to many,
Family, friends, lovers.
I opened my most sacred place to let them in.
I was fragile,
I was just starting to understand love.
I wasn't whole.
I opened my heart to ones I don't regret
But don't wish to remember.

I, never stopped loving."

"I've loved a lot of people in my life,
A lot more than I, to know
Everytime I tried to make someone's pain go
away,
Or help them find their purpose,
My sanity was to question.

I got lost trying to make sure they understood
their worth,
Without knowing my own."

I hear a lot of stories how someone's ex,
Or current partner is shitty,
But never hear the person taking accountability
for choosing to be with them through their toxic
behavior.

There are two sides to every story,
How can you play victim to something you keep
giving permission to?

Before I explain, I'm coming from a sincere place. A place of "I've been there, done that" so please, listen. I'm not speaking on physical abuse. I'm speaking on toxic relationships where the person keeps taking back the same person in their life.

You remember that time your friend dated someone you didn't like because they were no good for them? Well, this is pretty much that situation. You know their partner isn't what they deserve, as you have a front seat to their every breaking moment.

As an outsider looking in, it's easy to see the red flags and the signs they're so blinded by. You're not the one who loves them, so you see the picture as a whole and it's not a good one. The more advice you give to your friend the more they slip away from telling you what's going on. You get tired of hearing the same story. You've run out of helping hands to give once they cut you off from knowing about the relationship. Your advice isn't heard. Your concerns are overlooked with excuses. Your friend is in a mess and can't get themselves out.

Yes, this is toxic.

I want to be completely clear; someone can be in a toxic relationship without physical abuse. I feel like many people hear the word toxic and assume the worst possible thing. I'm not disregarding the fact there's a lot of cases of domestic violence, but this is my story and I can only speak from my experience and my view from the outside.

I, myself was in many toxic relations. I lost myself trying to be at their need. I gave up all my interests to fit into their lifestyle. I didn't see or go to family events because my partner had anxiety and didn't want to meet my family. He played his mental health on me and it made mine at an all-time high. I'm not downplaying his, we went out too many public outings. Concerts. Dinner. Movies. All his family events. I made excuses for him to my family, but once we were three years into the relationship and only met my parents twice, I thought there was a problem. I spent more time with him and his family I abandoned my own.

Yes, this is toxic on my part. I became comfortable with our life I didn't think I was being taken away from things I loved, because I lost the view. At the time, I didn't see it. There were days I would get upset, but I was never strong enough to leave. My ultimate scare was hurting him. In result, I only damaged myself.

I take full accountability for the lives I altered from the pain I caused.
I take full blame for the damage I did.
I take the fall for the ones who still can't admit to their doings on my heart.
I take the blame.

So, when I see someone going back to the same person who I know is no good. Who I see is hurting someone I love, I get why it's hard to walk away. What I don't get, is when they see them for who they truly are and take them back after seeing the person behind the mask.

Yes, there's a comfort in them they connect with. Or, it's the want of someone. The need of not feeling lonely. They'd rather have the disrespect, dishonesty and pain than be without someone.

That's what I don't get. Why see someone in their true colors and still take them back. When I tell you love isn't enough to hold someone close, it's not.

Someone who loves you won't treat your love like a game. They won't treat you terribly.

Someone who loves you, respects you.

Someone who loves you won't make you wonder if they do, they'll show you.

I know you're thinking,

"What happens when they show you, they love you, but then completely change" It's called the need. They need to get you, so they play you as their fool. They make you love them, so you'll be there when they need you.

Some people are cruel. Some people are so lost it can't be spoken. Some people are so damaged, not even you can fix them. You are not their therapist. You're not someone who holds their baggage. You are someone who deserves the love and respect you give. So please,

Don't take shit from anyone who treats you less. Take accountability for letting those overstay their welcome. Stop taking the same people back who only make you further from recognizing yourself. Don't let yourself get lost in their mask of love. Once they show they're not worthy, don't think twice,

JUST GO.

Family and Friends,

Is there a difference?

We're connected to family by blood. We grow either close to them or never knowing them. We're taught we need to stick by them, as if it's an obligation, when we don't owe them anything.

I grew up in a huge family. On my mother's side, my grandparents had 12 children. I'm not going to count how many cousins and great cousins. There's a lot. I grew close with a lot of them, some I never met. I grew around family "drama" and watching some of them get drunk and cause chaos. It was funny back then, but when I reflect, it's sad, to know their true intentions. I outgrew a lot of them. A lot of them don't deserve my energy. A lot of them don't know who they are, or where they're going. I pray they're always good. I don't associate with them whether we're related, or in other terms "blood" it's not a reason.

My twenties have been a huge learning journey for not only my inner self, but the person I surround myself with. I outgrew people I loved with a huge part of my heart, which includes family. I learned just because someone shares your blood doesn't make them a good person.

- It's okay to let go of family if they're toxic.
- It's okay to cut off anyone who doesn't treat you right.

Don't let anyone make you feel it's wrong just because your family.

Friends are connected through life,
We meet them in school, work, or online. We vibe with them off similar interests, or a personality match. Friends can stay for a long time or go as faster than the connection can grow. Friends can be family,
And family can make a best friend.
In result,
There's no need for a title,
You love who you love.

I've had friends who were more than family, and family members who are my best friends. It's all about connects and healthy communication. it's the soul that counts.

Family doesn't bleed loyalty,
They're can be fake as some 'friends.
You don't need to keep either close forever.

Don't be afraid to go ghost,

When you feel it's time to close the chapter.
Some people outlive their entitlement to an
explanation. Sometimes you did all you could,
said what you felt, and it still wasn't enough.

Sometimes silence is the explanation.
Sometimes silence brings us peace.

I condone "ghosting" behavior, only when you
communicated the issue multiple times and it
still wasn't resolved. There are only so many
chances you can give until there's no more hope
to have, or sanity left within you. If you feel you
gave all you could, to the point you're now
taking away from you, walk away. I mean that
without hesitation. They don't care enough to
change their toxic ways after admitting to those
traits. Don't care enough to hold onto them. No
matter the years spent, if it takes a toll on your
mental health, LET IT GO. The love will always
stay in your heart, but their presence won't be
the same. Sometimes you need to love from afar.
Some people don't deserve an explanation on
why they keep damaging your heart. if they
don't see it, don't bother. Choose you.

<u>Someone asked me to write about the love we almost had…</u>

I remember wondering what we could be, I became accustomed to my fantasy of us. I couldn't see the real presented in front of me. I couldn't blame you for the tragedy my heart was left with for years to come after the loss of you. I couldn't blame you for not loving me the way I thought you would. I couldn't blame you for hiding the truth from me because I would have found a reason to not believe you. The lies kept me around. The mystery of what we could have been had me high, too high, I couldn't imagine coming down. I couldn't imagine being without you, and I, didn't even have you. I blamed you for a lot of the scars that came with our ending. Back then, when I was young and naïve, I blame you for misleading me. You could have walked away once you saw the love bleed through me for you, but you chose to hold me close and play me as your fool. I blame you for continuing to hurt me, as you had every moment to confess. We weren't meant to be, that I, saw a future envisioned you couldn't give me. I spent four years giving you everything I could, I don't blame you for that. I blame myself for trying to force something the universe kept taking away from me. I couldn't blame you for all the times I came back hoping this one time may be ours. So, I don't blame you for our tragedy. I can't even blame myself. We both played our parts. I was once bitter towards the thought of you, now, I'm aware of why I had to love you so deeply and why I had to lose you. The best thing about you, Even though you couldn't love me, You showed me what love isn't, You brought me the best gift, The road to self.

"Sex is fun,
But without an intimate connection
It's only a temporary void.

Someone who knows your body's language,
That's a soulmate,
Someone who matches your love language,
Brings you comfort
And brings out the freak in you,
Irreplaceable."

Outgrowing old habits,
Old friends,
Old lovers
Is a part of life.

Stop thinking that growing apart from someone means the worst outcome. Stop holding together what's already broken, there's no mending together what's already gone.

When you force any kind of relationship, with anyone that's not meant to go on any longer will only result in more pain. Stop letting pain grow within situations you should have let go long ago. Wake up, don't hold on when they've already let go.

Letting go is one of the hardest things, as you planted the idea in your head from the beginning. Look at it like this, letting go is beautiful. Especially when it's become toxic to you. Letting go of the old and welcome the happiness behind the misery.

I've found beauty while outgrowing people I've loved for most of my lifetime. Finding love in letting them go, to give myself the love I wished they could have given me. Self-love is the most important lesson of it all.

"Sex without a connection,
Is a temporary high.
Coming down will leave you emptier.
There's something magical
In sharing your heart, body and soul
With someone who genuinely loves you.
Someone who takes the time
To learn every part of you."

The thought of losing someone you love is a scary thought.

But, why think about losing someone who isn't leaving? The illusions you create of someone leaving you, and how love is painful, the more you're going to believe those illusions.

Just love and let yourself be loved.

The illusions that love is painful, love is scary, is just in your head. Love is many things, neither painful nor scary. When you're in love with someone who loves you back, nothing about that is painful. If you feel this way, you're in love with the wrong one.

In my past I thought I was in love many times. I thought I met my twin flame, but I was entirely wrong. I loved with my whole heart and in the moment, I thought they were the one. It felt right. But when you truly fall, all those old loves won't feel like love at all.

I fell for the need of finding love, not the person. I fell in love with the thought of being in love and being loved back. I attached anyone to that because I was a hopeless romantic. I was in love with the idea of love.

"You can't disconnect from me
And expect me not to grow without you."

"I became distant with souls
I never wanted to live without,
That's when I found comfort in being alone."

Write a letter to an old friend

_____

_____

_____

_____

_____

_____

_____

_____

_____

_____

_____

_____

_____

_____

_____

_____

Write a letter to an ex

_____

_____

_____

_____

_____

_____

_____

_____

_____

_____

_____

_____

_____

_____

Write a letter to the you that got lost in love

_____

_____

_____

_____

_____

_____

_____

_____

_____

_____

_____

_____

_____

_____

_____

What's a healthy relationship to you?

_____

_____

_____

_____

_____

_____

_____

_____

_____

_____

_____

_____

_____

_____

_____

Be honest, what's your toxic trait?

How did you overcome it?

_____

_____

_____

_____

_____

_____

_____

_____

_____

_____

_____

_____

_____

_____

_____

Thank you for giving my work a chance. I pray you chose to get this book to feel what I had to offer from my experience. I know it's not probably exactly what you wish to hear, but it's the truth I've discovered along my journey. It took me some time to withhold this information for it to stick. I don't wish heartbreak on anyone because the pain stings terribly, but it gives us strength. I hope you found that within reading. I hope you found the beauty in letting go, or soon realize. Come back to this book whenever you need reminders. Highlight. Write notes.

Take care of you,
Every relationship that comes to you will test you. Don't let them define you.

Book pictures are appreciated,
Highly recommended!

If you enjoyed,
Feel free to leave a review on Amazon or
Goodreads. Love to hear your feedback.

For more of my work:

Email: moonsoulchild@outlook.com
Instagram: @moonsoulchild
Twitter @moonssoulchild
Facebook @moonsoulchild

Made in the USA
Monee, IL
04 June 2020